Data Analytics

The Ultimate Beginner's Guide to Data Analytics

by Edward Mize

Table of Contents

Who is this book for?

Within the discipline of data analytics, we cannot neglect the importance of the mathematical discipline, which often deals with the analysis or examination of numbers. This is called statistical methods.

In fact, the fundamental basis of data analytics concerns the use of these methods.

The data analytics methods have an important role, and everyone considers them as the most used techniques in both developed and advanced countries. Actually, this method is not to be overlooked.

For example, almost all multi-national companies and leading industries, use this kind of method for rapid prototyping and research and development.

A large knowledge of these two methods (Statistical Analysis and Data Analytics) is incredibly advantageous, and this prompted us to create this book.

It is intended for beginners who are interested in the practice of data analytics.

This book has been made for students, researchers, and anyone who wants to learn the use of this famous new method, and especially for people who are passionate about statistical analysis.

This book is intended for students who have chosen statistical analysis as part of their course of study.

What will this book teach you?

This book will be useful for students wishing to deepen their knowledge in the practical method of statistical analysis or data analytics, and will contribute to their initial training as a data analyst.

This book provides only introductory subjects for the discipline in the field of data technology.

The basis of this work is the theory of mathematical model ling, illustrated by the different calculations used within statistical analysis.

The purpose of this book is to lead readers in formulating and solving questions using statistical analysis or data analytics.

The importance of this book is to understand the main concepts of statistical analysis and the data analytic methods. This should be undertaken prior to attempting the various problems that may be met in each area.

Introduction

Currently, many people know about data analytics.

Almost all sectors of activity, and various fields of production, or enterprises use this new method in order to promote, develop, and to facilitate the technique of working, evaluation, and of course, the future state of their projects.

In fact, it is useful in the progression or the development of many companies - in the commercial sector or the field of marketing, finance, banking, as well as certain industries using computers as a primary tool.

All of these entities use this method through specialists and experts with data analytical skills with the aim to find a rapid and permanent development. In other words, the method of data analysis is currently ubiquitous.

In fact, talking about data analytics seems to speak also with a competence on the field of statistics, in particular, on the method of analysis used by statistics.

In addition, the method of analysis is called statistical analysis or statistical data analysis.

Therefore, the analysis of information is based on the background of statistics and probabilities, whether by means of computers or not.

In this case, a mathematics discipline is a fundamental tool for this method.

Consequently, data analytic specialists are called analysts or data scientists.

On the other hand, the data analytics method is a thorough analysis of a new proven knowledge, rational and treated, through the application of the data analytics method.

The use of the data analytics method in the domain of health is also very crucial.

Data analytics is also used by many hospitals, medical institutes and laboratories.

Such methods are very important for medical researchers, for instance, in the field of epidemiology.

It is extremely useful for mastering several data recording methods, and facilitates the technique of analysis that physicians or medical experts use.

In fact, science depends largely on data analytics methods.

Chapter 1: The Meaning of Data Analytics Method

The Fundamental Definitions Concerning the Data Analytics Method

The Term "Analysis"

The term analysis is known by everyone, as the decomposition of a body, of a substance into its constituent elements, or a study made to discern the different parts of a whole, to determine or explain the relationship with each other.

To analyse is to consider the relationship between data and data sets.

For example, financial analysis, mathematical analysis, computer analysis, etc.

The Term "Data"

With regards to the word "data", these are fundamental elements of meaning, which serve as a basis for reasoning, research, and especially for a well-defined analysis.

Data can be a combination of objects, numbers, images, turnovers, etc., chosen by their quality, their rarity, their character, their value, or their price.

Consider some examples: a collection of stamps, currencies, numbers representing a fact, or a set of models created to make an analytical tool.

Most data is put into digital form. That means a conventional representation of information in a form suitable for computer processing.

In addition, the data is part of the basic idea that serves as a starting point for an analysis.

Data Analysis or Data Analytics

From what we have seen above, data analysis or data analytics can be defined as a thorough study of a well-defined collection.

This is made in order to draw a relevant conclusion after having visualized and interpreted the various research on the relationship between the data in one, or multiple statistical tables.

If we want to go further, it is also a piece of work showing a detailed study of a problem. Additionally, they are predictions based on existing data in order to make reliable and useful decisions, and to avoid difficult or dangerous problems.

In other words, data analytics is a lot of hard work, requiring specific skills.

The General Purpose of Data Analytics Method

The main objective of data analytics is to cite or to explicit reliable solutions to the observed problems on the relationships and interdependencies between processed data, after using statistical tables or graphical representations of data.

The Data Analysts

Data analysts are people who specialize in data analysis.

For instance, those who work within finance and banking, and are experts of data analytics are called financial analysts.

In the area of statistical analysis, the experts of data analytics are called statisticians.

In politics, the experts of data analytics are called law analysts, and finally, in the area of informatics and computers, the experts are called analyst programmers or business analysts.

Generally, data analysts are experts in statistical analysis. They are familiar to managing, evaluating and interpreting the meanings presented in the results tables of a complex analysis.

The Different Tasks Performed by Data Analysts

The following are the different tasks that data analysts perform, in every area of their work:

Analysts Programmer

- These are developers of computer programs within business. Specialists are called business analysts.

Specialist in finance and banking data management

- They are called financial analysts.

The skills of data analysts

Data analysis is directly related to statistical analysis.

As result, a general knowledge on the topic of statistics is indispensable. Ideally this should be at least at the level of a second year mathematics undergraduate student.

As its name indicates, a data analyst is a person responsible for:

- The handling of quantitative data
- The statistical studies of data collections
- The updating of a data collection through using a spreadsheet or a database
- Within sensitive areas, the data analyst may be responsible for the security of the data

Required Diploma and University Curriculum

Firstly, a data analyst has a passion for statistics.

For this, some knowledge of computer science and statistical skills are indispensable.

The required skills for becoming a data analyst normally begins at masters degree level.

For example, a Master's Degree in Computer Science and Applied Statistics, Applied Statistics in Data Analysis and Computer engineering are the most common.

The remuneration of a data analyst can reach the value of $3000 per month, for new entrants. However, this amount may vary depending on the experience and qualifications. For a data science expert, the amount can reach $3500 to $4000.

Basic Terms Frequently Used in Data Analytics

Data

These are collections of images, sounds, numbers, text and suchlike.

Database

A database is a well-defined and structured information set that is stored in computer equipment.

DBMS

The DBMS or database management system is software for storing and processing information from the database.

The following are examples of database management systems: Oracle, MySQL, JAVA DB, Microsoft SQL Server and Microsoft Access.

Big Data

Big data is a massive data set, which can only be processed through using computer tools due to its complexity.

Data Mining

Data mining is a set of analytical tools used to extract information from multiple data sources.

Data Warehouse

A data warehouse is a large store of data accumulated from a wide range of sources within a company and is used to guide management decisions.

What Is the Use of Data Analytics?

Based on what we have seen above, the data analytics process involves studies, research, as well as an exploration of information.

Data analytics are used to examine and interpret data collections in order to obtain and understand the data, and to analyze it in order to come to a conclusion.

To do this, it is very important to understand the theory and application of statistical methods.

Indeed, the process of data analysis is frequently made by observing complex relationships. Often these are between the different kinds of data presented in huge tables. The interpretation of the results are undertaken through calculations of various parameters, such as correlations, variances, and covariances.

To conclude, data analysis involves the transformation of data into useful information. Subsequently, this results in better decision making.

The Different Parts of The Data Analytics Method

Data analysis may be carried out by performing the following steps:

- The identification of the research to be carried out or the study concerned by the analysis. This includes the definition and description of the data to be collected.

- The definition of the problems to be analyzed and objectives to be achieved

- The data collection methodology. The definition of the information or collected data, the location, and the purpose of the analysis.

- The definition of the data source

- The data processing (analysis and interpretation of results)

- The presentation of the results

It is important to follow these steps in any study.

To do this, the analyst must be fair and accurate in carrying out these tasks, as all this is part of the data analytical approach.

The Method of Data Analytics and Computing

The method of data analytics and computing are inseparable.

This is due to the current representation of the form of the data sources.

Since all data is in digital form, intuitively, any database will be in digital form too.

As a result, computer literacy is essential to the practice of the data analytics method.

Data analysis is usually accomplished through using a computer. For instance, the data to be analyzed must be processed by the computer in its extraction, processing of raw data, transformations, etc.

Before launching the research and the method of analysis, an analyst must be skilled in computer use.

Data Analysis and Statistic Methods

The practice of data analytics requires knowledge of applied mathematics, both in statistics and probability. In most cases, data analysis is related to the statistical analysis method.

The latter currently uses a lot of scientific processing software, which computers interpret and do automatic analysis with.

These programs replace the work and mathematically process the calculations that the data analysts do.

An understanding of mathematics is required for the application of this method.

The calculations and the graphical representations take place more during the analysis process.

Statistical Analysis and Data Analytics Method

As we know, statistics is a part of applied mathematics and the analytical study of digital data (accounting, processing, estimation, correlation study, etc.) which aims to give rational and easy results that can be used by any analytical method or research study.

Sometimes, statistics methods are considered as a science of enumeration, but in fact, it is an important tool used for data analytics.

It is also a basic method for any analytical tasks. Obviously, a data analyst is automatically an expert in the field of statistics.

The statistical method describes and explains large-scale tables to visualize and interpret certain aspects of data.

Statistical Software for The Data Analytics Method

Some data needs specific tools for processing or analysis, for example in the case of big data.

Software tools can be very helpful and improve the expected results after the initial analysis.

Here is some software frequently used in statistical data analysis:

Microsoft Office Excel and XLSTAT

Known by everyone, Excel is a piece of software in the form of a spreadsheet, and the first software used by statistical data analysts, thus also indispensable for data analytics.

Excel allows us to process a multitude of data, by using different functions and specific formulas, as well as providing graphical representations.

Moreover, Excel is the first programmable spreadsheet thanks to its inbuilt language called VBA (Visual Basic Applications).

For example, qualitative and quantitative statistical variables analysis, whether univariate or bivariate, can be performed with Excel.

In addition, Excel can be much stronger when it is used with XLSTAT. This is a statistical analysis add on for Excel. XLSTAT is compatible with any version of Excel.

STATA

This is specific econometric software used in the analysis of epidemiological and economic data.

A French statistician called William Gould created STATA software. This software excels in the automatic management of massive databases. In addition, the STATA commands are easy to master (for example - use, in-file, sheet, etc.)

SPSS

SPSS stands for Statistical Package for Social Sciences. SPSS is the software used in statistical analysis by data analysis.

SPSS has the following components: IBM, SPSS-modeler, statistic analytic server, etc. SPSS also can also be used for the execution of some data analysis process steps in statistics (for example, modelling, database management, big- data study, reporting, etc.).

SAS

As the other previous applications, SAS is extremely popular as statistical software, and is used by data analysts and statisticians.

SAS is a language used especially in statistics. SAS stands for Statistical Analysis System.

In terms of programming, it is sometimes called SAS / STAT.
This software is considered to be the software used specifically in the analysis of descriptive and / or predictive statistics.

Additionally, a set of processes, or a database, can be created, processed, and managed easily with SAS.

In fact, SAS is not only data analysis software, but it is also a programming language to facilitate the analytical study of a search or data processing.

It is compatible with many operating systems such as windows or Linux.

R

R is also known as RSTAT

The data processing and analysis software R is also a special programming language used in statistical analysis.

Analysts know this software as a very sophisticated and useful statistical software package.

What differentiates R from other data analysis software is its standard aspect on integration with statistical analysis.

Additional Point to Note

Before carrying out a statistical analysis of data, the following points should be checked:

- Check and justify the areas to be analyzed

- Identify the data characteristics with faults or anomalies (for example incomplete, defective data etc.)

- Make a table representing the data to be examined

- Make the study or certain statistical parameters (averaging, standard deviation, minimum and maximum values) from data represented by the table

- Choose the types of flowchart to be established after observing the statistical tables representing the relations between the data

- Choose the statistical tests to be applied (use of calculation of the coefficient of variation, R^2, Eta^2, etc...)

- Interpret and give an explanation for the observed data relationships in the graphic representations or tables

The Principal Scope of The Data Analytics Method

A multitude of data can be processed, analyzed and outputted through using statistical analytical software.

From this data, we can identify new ideas, often represented by graphs.

Mathematics and computer science are two indispensable disciplines in the practice of this method.

At present, almost all sectors of activity and fields of work who use the data analytics method utilize statistical software as well as experts in data analysis.

Here are some examples:

Medical and health fields, banking, public finance field, and sector marketing. There is also commercial, journalism, scientific research, anthropology, archaeology, computer science, and statistics.

Students, or anyone interested in joining this discipline, are expected to have long-term, excellent, and progressive careers, as all sectors are influenced by this method

Read This FIRST - 100% FREE BONUS

FOR A LIMITED TIME ONLY – Get the best-selling book *"5 Steps to Learn Absolutely Anything in as Little As 3 Days!"* by TeachingNerds absolutely FREE!

Readers who have read this bonus book as well have seen huge increases in their abilities to learn new things and apply it to their lives – so it is *highly recommended* to get this bonus book.

Once again, as a big thank-you for downloading this book, I'd like to offer it to you *100% FREE for a LIMITED TIME ONLY!*

To download your FREE copy, go to:

<u>TeachingNerds.com/Bonus</u>

Chapter 2: The Different Types of The Data Analytics Method

General Viewpoint

The types and processes of the method of data analysis depend on the nature of the analysis to be performed.

In fact, the types of analysis that often occur are the quantitative analysis method and the qualitative analysis method.

For this purpose, this chapter will observe the different stages of the two fundamental methods.

The Principal Component Analysis (PCA)

PCA stands for Principal Component Analysis.

The Principal Component Analysis is a technique used in data analytics, whose objective is the transformation of two, or several, correlated statistical variables, to obtain new variables, which are not interconnected.

This method is often applied to the multivariate statistical variables. The term Principal Component means "uncorrelated statistical variables".

During the practice of the PCA, the fundamental analysis of statistical regression and correlation is used.

Consequently, this method requires the mastery of the various mathematical formulas used in statistics (linear regression, calculation of correlations between variables, etc.)

The Principal Component Analysis method uses certain mathematical formulas.

Therefore, an accurate background of the notion of space vectors and that of matrices (matrix of covariance, correlation matrix) are used to make a reduction in the dimensions of space, which we use in the method to do a reduction of the elements in a basic set of data.

In the most general case, the analysis is mainly dependent upon the study and interpretation of p −dimensional graphs ($p \geq 3$).

So, if we want to accomplish a Principal Component Analysis, certain mathematical formulas must be mastered, because statistical parameters depend on such rules.

The Advantage of The Application of PCA Method

This method is effective for, and also compatible with, the treatment of large sets of data.

Also, the Principal Component Analysis may be considered as a technique of detection and reduction of statistical variables in the case of statistical redundancy.

The use of PCA facilitates the control of parameters that represent the character of each relevant indicator.

Even if the observed results are large, they are easily understandable after interpreting the graph from a PCA.

Nevertheless, there are some disadvantages using this method.

For example, the method is not reliable for identifying different kinds of variances.

The Correspondence Factor Analysis (CFA)

CFA, or Correspondence Factor Analysis, is an analytical method used in data analysis, and was created by a French statistician.

With this method, the analysis of data is carried out by means of the multivariate analysis technique, and involves multivariate statistical study.

Generally, the CFA method describes and explains the relationship between two statistical variables.

It also visualizes the internal relationships between the variables and provides a new aspect of the statistical population.

The Correspondence Factor Analysis is divided into two main parts. The part of the descriptive statistical analysis method, and the explanatory method.

What differentiates this method from other statistical analysis techniques is that it is based on the method of analytical data.

The meaning of the different scatters observed in the graphic representation is important for the data interpretation observed on statistics tables.

The CFA, makes it possible to determine the results between two qualitative statistical variables.

Finally, this method also highlights the existence study of contingency tables and the so-called chi-squared test denoted by $\chi 2$.

The Contingency Table

The contingency table is a special statistical table which serves to simultaneously represent data of two individuals of a single statistical population.

In most cases, the data is represented by an array of double entries.

The distance $\chi 2$ (chi-squared) of the contingency, or also metric $\chi 2$, is one of the statistical tests used in data analytics.

This test is carried out with a specific calculation, using a mathematical formula, whose purpose is to verify whether two statistical variables are dependent or independent.

For example, if the result of the calculation of $\chi 2$ is equal to 0, the two variables are independent of each other.

Correspondence Factor Analysis

The Correspondence Factor Analysis allows the analysis to be undertaken in one scatter diagram even if the data sample is quite large.

The CFA can highlight certain elements called correspondences, which cannot be calculated directly numerically.

The Multiple Correspondence Analysis (or MCA)

Multiple Correspondence Analysis is a method used in statistical analysis to study the link between two or more statistical variables.

CFA is considered to be a type of MCA.

Within Correspondence Factor Analysis, the study of the relationship is between two variables, but where this number exceeds the value of two, then it is better to use Multiple Correspondence Analysis.

The CFA concerns the analysis of qualitative variables.

The same applies to the case of the MCA, whereas the PCA concerns mainly quantitative statistical analysis.

The fundamental principle of the MCA is to have two tables called the disjunctive table and the Burt table. This is after having described qualitative variables, which are also shown in tables.

Therefore, it is an interpretation of obtained results from disjointed tables representing qualitative data values.

The Burt table is a statistical table, allowing us to observe qualitative variable studies - the purpose of which is to facilitate the study of the data by calculation.

Such a table is more often used in the CFA and MCA data analysis.
Since MCA is the general case of the CFA, this method is also related to the study of scatter diagrams, and the various calculations that remain valid.

The aim of the MCA is also to determine the correlation between the several statistical modalities.

In this case, the qualitative data is represented by a special table, which is called a complete disjunctive table.

In this table, the lines are considered as individuals, and columns represent the modalities of the qualitative variables.

The Advantage of MCA Practice

The first observed benefit of applying this method is that this analysis is used in several surveys, which are made using multiple techniques.

In addition, the MCA is considered to be a reduced form of the method called multiple factor analysis, or mixed analysis.

Comparison Between CFA, MCA and PCA

According to the PCA analytical study, in most of the cases, the statistical variables to be studied are one quantitative variable, whereas with the CFA studies, it is about two qualitative variables.

In any case, the MCA is just a generalization of the CFA, because it is an analytical study for more than two qualitative variables.

The data analytics of these three types of analysis (CFA, MCA and PCA) constitutes what is called a multiple factorial analysis.

Chapter 3: Application of Statistics with The Data Analytics

Generalities

First of all, defining the types of analysis to be used is very important in statistical analysis.

For each type of analysis, we also need a good choice of tools that can be used with the statistical method.

For any method of data analysis, a statistical background is always indispensable.

The statistical analysis is mainly performed by the practice of two analytical methods: qualitative analysis and quantitative analysis.

The option to use these types depends on the nature of the data to be analyzed.

Definition of Statistics

Statistics is a discipline in general mathematics that is interested in data collection studies or information, by means of calculations, enumerations, or estimates.

It is a study of a characteristic or aspect of an event, a circumstance or situation, through the use of a specific analytical method.

This method depends on the use of computers, because the data that statistics experts use are currently almost always in digital form.

Statistics are considered a part of the most used applied mathematics. Indeed, the principle of probability is a part of the analytical complement in the case of inferential statistics.

Basic Terms Used in Statistical Analysis

The terms frequently used in statistical analysis are as follows:

- **Statistical population**

  The statistical population of a special set of data where in elements are called individual.

- **Statistical individual**

  An element of the statistical population.

- **Statistical sample**

  It is a part of the population set (ie., subset of the population).

- **Descriptive statistics**

  This is a part of the statistical analysis describing a set of statistical parameters by means of the methods of data analysis (mean, standard deviation, correlation coefficient).

- **Inferential statistics**

This is a statistical method which allows estimating the parameter(s) of a set of individuals.

- **Statistical variable**

This is a value or character to be studied in statistics.

The variable is called qualitative if the considered values are not quantifiable (uncountable values, for example: the character to be studied is a color).

The variable is called quantitative if the considered values are quantifiable, or numerical (countable, continuous or discontinuous variable).

- **Statistical series**

The set of values of the individuals or characters to be studied.

The statistical series may be discrete or non-discrete (in the case of a continuous series).

- **Statistical Series with Two Variables (Bivariate Descriptive Statistics)**

Firstly, the two-variable statistical series concerns the quantitative statistical variable. In that case, the characters to be studied are two in number, each of which is represented by number.

The statistical series with two variables are usually represented by X and Y, which indicate the different Statistical Inference or Inferential Statistics.

- **Inferential Statistics**

  Inferential statistics is a statistical study whose analysis of data is based on the study of a set of characters forming a part of the statistical population called the sample.

  Inferential statistics is, therefore, a method whereby a random sample of data is taken in order to represent the whole.

  With this method, data analytics concerns the descriptive statistics and depends as well on the evaluation of probability calculation. This is based mainly on the study of the estimate and statistical hypothesis testing.

  Therefore, a detailed knowledge of probability indispensable in inferential statistics.

The Different Statistical Parameters Used in Data Analysis

The expected results of statistical work are tables or a graph.

It is on the basis of such results that we can deduce conclusions or interpret certain observations, in order to arrive at a single objective: the result of the analysis.

To do this, some calculations using statistical formulas must be carried out.

These formulas are often called statistical parameters. We will evaluate, in this chapter, the notion of these parameters.

The statistical parameters are divided into two parts: the dispersion parameters and position parameters.

The position parameters are defined by the median and the arithmetic mean. The dispersion parameters are represented by the quartiles, the interquartile range, the extended R, the standard deviation, variances, and the coefficient of variation.

Since data analytics use the statistical method, the statistical parameters are used for the completion of such an analysis.

As we have seen in the previous chapters, if the data is of a qualitative nature, we apply the method of statistical analysis to qualitative variables, and in the case of a quantitative nature, the quantitative statistical analysis technique is used.

Statistical Analysis with Qualitative Variable

The qualitative analysis of data is a study of data whose basic principle consists of examining a set of qualitative or non-countable data.

For example, it is impossible to count the aspects of color, or the characteristic of a study. A study concerning such aspects should be done qualitatively through the analysis and study of their quality.

The purpose of qualitative research is to investigate aspects, behaviors, or perceptive facts of a given statistical individual aspect, with a study much deeper than that of a survey.

Qualitative variable analysis can also be called exploratory analysis.

The Quantitative Analysis Method

The method of quantitative data analysis consists of examining a finite number, by means of characteristics analysis, opinions, or behaviors, thanks to the use of method of sampling.

This method may be contrary to that of qualitative analysis, but sometimes they are additional.

Quantitative analysis is used in many areas or sectors (finance, economics, science, etc.), and it is based on the available data.

The aspects of the character to be studied must be quantifiable.

Linear Adjustment Technique

With the statistical method, linear adjustment is a method used for predicting or estimating specific values.

Linear adjustment technique is necessary for the adjustment of a few points in order to give an appearance or similarity, as close as possible to a linear line.

Linear adjustment is used in a two-variable statistical series.

In the most commonly used case, adjustment techniques consist of studying the relations between two or more statistical variables by the representation of scatters.

In reality, adjustment is the action of changing. As for the statistical analysis, it is a matter of transforming the scatters to give a form closer to the graph of the linear function $y = ax + b$.

There are two methods for finding the adjustment: the Mayer's method, or the least squares method.

The Least Squares Method

The least squares method is a linear fitting method whose main goal is to find a line closer to an affine function by means of calculus: the difference between the theoretical and experimental points.

The Mayer's Method

The Mayer's method is a technique whose aim is to adjust the scatter points by sharing it with two simple groups, and then determining a special point called the mean point.

The Linear Regression

Regression analysis is a statistical method used to study the relationship between a dependent variable, and one or more independent variables.

It is the study of the interdependencies between two variables with different characteristics.

Such a relation is always performed with the form of a linear function. That is why the method is called linear regression.

For this, we have: $y = f(x)$, where is the independent variable and y that of the dependent.

When the variable x is unique, we say that the regression analysis is called bivariate, and it is called multiple in the case where the variable could be more than one value.

Mathematically, the regression line is expressed as $y = ax + b$.

We can take the following example: the wealth that a person can own depends on the amount of his money. We can assume variable x as the amount of money, and variable y as the fortune.

Consequently, we have: $fortune = f\ (money)$. If the value of money increases or falls, the capacity of fortune changes.

Therefore, in our case, there is a linear dependence between fortune and money.

They are in a relationship. A study of this using the statistical method is called linear regression analysis.

The Linear or Linear Regression Line of Least Squares

The aim in this study is to adjust the data represented in the given equation of the type $y = ax + b$.

Let $M_i\ (x_i,\ y_i)$ be the points forming the scatter, and $Ni\ (x_i,\ ax_i + \beta)$ the additional points for the adjustment.

It is assumed that the pair (α, β) minimizes the function $f(a, b)$ such that

$$f(a, b) = \sum_{i \in \mathbb{N}} (y_i - ax_i - b)^2$$

The regression line of y in x is given by the equation $y = \alpha x + \beta$

Where $\alpha = \dfrac{cov\ (X,Y)}{\sigma_X}$ and that $\beta = \bar{y} + \alpha\bar{x}$

The mean for the variable X

$$\bar{x} = \frac{1}{n} \sum_{1 \leq i \leq n} x_i$$

and

The mean for the variable Y

$$\bar{y} = \frac{1}{n} \sum_{1 \leq i \leq n} y_i$$

Besides, the covariance of X and Y formula is

$$cov\ (X,Y) = \frac{1}{n-1} \sum_{1 \leq i \leq n} (x_i - \bar{x})(y_i - \bar{y})$$

The coefficient of correlation

The coefficient of correlation is the number defined by r such that

$$r = \frac{cov\ (X,Y)}{\sigma_X\ \sigma_Y}$$

Where

$$\sigma_X = \sqrt{\frac{1}{n-1} \sum_{1 \leq i \leq n} (x_i - \bar{x})^2}$$

and

$$\sigma_Y = \sqrt{\frac{1}{n-1} \sum_{1 \leq i \leq n} (y_i - \bar{y})^2}$$

σ_X and σ_Y are respectively the standard deviation of X and Y

This number r must be between -1 and 1. X and Y are statistical variables.

In fact, this number is used to explain certain links between the variables X and Y.

It is also a linear adjustment method because the calculus purpose is to find an equation of a straight line.

The Various Statistical Tests

Talking about a statistical analysis is similar to talking about statistical testing.

Statistical tests are techniques used in statistical methods and data analytics, to accept or reject, with a certain risk of errors, an assumption relating to the statistical population or the probability chosen to represent the sample.

Such a process is made from a function of observations, with one or more samples of statistical population.

The decision making after the test process depends on the characteristic of a statistical axiom called null hypothesis.

Statistical tests are divided into two main parts: parametric tests and nonparametric tests.

Parametric testing is a test used in the analysis of data concerning the distribution law, so, it concerns some rules from probability studies as well.

The Basic Parametric Tests

In fact, there exists several types of statistical test and hypothesis, but we only need some examples.

Parametric test examples are:

The student test, the test of Hartley, Anova, etc.

The nonparametric test uses no axiom or hypothesis for the adjustment test.

Example of nonparametric tests:

The Dixon test, Wihaxon test, kolmogorov-simirov test, etc.

Sometimes factorial analysis is called ANOVA, which stands for Analysis of Variances.

Other than the student tests, there are also χ^2 tests (chi squared test), the Fisher test, the median tests etc.

Chapter 4: Mathematics Courses Most Used in Data Analytics

Notion of The Space Vector

Rings

Let E be a set provided with two laws of internal composition $+$ (addition) and $\times$ (multiplication). The triplet $(E, +, \times)$ is called Ring if the following axioms are satisfied:

- $\forall\, a \in E$ $\quad a$ is called "vector"
- $\forall\, (a, b) \in E^2$ $\quad a + b = b + a$
- $\forall\, (a, b, c) \in E^3 (a + b) + c = a + (b + c)$
- $\exists\, 0_A \in E, \forall\, a \in E \quad a + 0_E = a$
- $\forall\, a \in E, \exists\, a' \in E \quad a + a' = 0_E,$
  in this case $a' = -a$
- $\forall\, (a, b, c) \in E^3 (a \times b) \times c = a \times (b \times c)$
- $\forall\, (a, b, c) \in E^3 (a + b) \times c = (a \times c) + (b \times c)$
- $\forall\, (a, b, c) \in E^3 \quad a \times (b + c) = (a \times b) + (a \times c)$

If the law $(+)$ is commutative, E is called commutative ring.

If the law $(\times)$ has a neutral element 1_E, E is called a unit ring.

For example, the set of integers, real numbers, rational numbers and especially complex numbers are rings.

The Invertible Elements

Let $(E, +, \times)$ be a unit ring. An element $a \in E$ is an invertible element if there exists a' such that $a' \in E$, and $a \times a' = 1_E$

a' is called the inverse of a.

The Field K

Let K be a set provided with two laws of internal composition $+$ (addition) and x (multiplication). The set K is called a field if:

$(K, +)$ is a commutative group

$(K, +, \times)$ is a unit ring

For all element a of $K *= K - \{0\}$, a is invertible (for the law of the multiplication)

Briefly, if the ring is commutative, then K is a commutative field.

The Vector Space

In the following case, K is a field which can be assumed as $\mathbb{R}$ or $\mathbb{C}$.

The set $(E, +, \times)$ is a vector space over K ($\mathbb{R}$ or $\mathbb{C}$) or simply K-vector space, if the following axioms are satisfied:

- $(E, +, \times)$ *is an unit ring*
- $\forall\, \lambda \in R,\, \forall\, a \in E \quad \lambda \times a = \lambda.a$
- $\forall\, \lambda \in R, \forall\, \omega \in R, \forall\, a \in E(\lambda + \omega) \times a = (\lambda \times a) + (\omega \times a)$
- $\forall\, \lambda \in R, \forall\, (a, b) \in E^2 \quad \lambda \times (a \times b) = (\lambda \times a) \times b = (\lambda \times b) \times a$
- $\forall\, \omega \in R, \forall\, (a, b) \in E^2 \quad \omega \times (a + b) = (\omega \times a) + (\omega \times b)$

Examples:

$(\mathbb{R}^2, +, \times)$ is a space vector, such that:

- $(a, b) + (a', b') = (a + a', b + b')$
- $(a, b) \times (a', b') = (aa' - bb', ab' + ba')$

When $E = \mathbb{R}^n$, for all $n \in \mathbb{N}^*$

The addition law is defined as:

$$(x_1, x_2, \ldots, x_n) + (y_1, y_2, \ldots, y_n) = (x_1 + y_1, x_2 + y_2, \ldots x_n + y_n)$$

The multiplication law is defined as:

$\forall\, \lambda \in R,\ \forall\, a \in E \quad a = (x_1, x_2, \ldots, x_n),$ we have
$\lambda a = (\lambda x_1, \lambda x_2, \ldots, \lambda x_n)$

In fact, $(\mathbb{R}^2, +, \times)$ is a space vector over $\mathbb{R}$.

$E = M_2(\mathbb{R})$ is the set of square matrices of order 2, with a real coefficients.

$E = M_2(\mathbb{R})$ is a space vector over R.

Remark

$$\forall \lambda \in R, \qquad \forall a \in E \qquad \lambda \times a = \lambda . a = \lambda a$$

$\forall a \in E \quad 1a = a$, and if $a = 0$, a is called zero vector.

The Zero Divisors

Let $(E, +, \times)$ be a commutative ring

For all $(a, b) \in E^2$, such that a and b are satisfying the following conditions:

$$a \neq 0, b \neq 0 \text{ and } a \times b = 0_E$$

In this case, a and b are zero divisors of the commutative ring.

System of Vectors

Let $(E, +, \times)$ be a space vector over K ($\mathbb{R}$ or $\mathbb{C}$).

The system of n vectors $(a_1, a_2, \ldots, a_n)$ of E is the set denoted by
$$S = (a_1, a_2, \ldots, a_n).$$

In this case, S is a set of n order.

Linear Combination of Vectors

The Linear combination of vectors $(a_1, a_2, \ldots, a_n)$ whose coefficients are respectively $\lambda_1, \lambda_2, \ldots, \lambda_n$ is the vector b, such that:

$$b = \lambda_1 a_1 + \lambda_2 a_2 + \cdots + \lambda_n a_n$$

The Linearly Independent Vectors

The system of n vectors $(a_1, a_2, \ldots, a_n)$ of E is called linearly independent vectors, if the following implication is satisfied:

$$b = \lambda_1 a_1 + \lambda_2 a_2 + \cdots + \lambda_n a_n = 0$$

implies

$$\lambda_1 = \lambda_2 = \cdots = \lambda_n = 0$$

Dimension of The Space Vector

Let $(E, +, \times)$ be a space vector over K ($\mathbb{R}$ or $\mathbb{C}$)

The dimension of E over K is the order n of all basis of E

For example:

When $E = \mathbb{R}^n$, for all $n \in \mathbb{N}^*$ $(\mathbb{R}^n, +, \times)$ is a space vector over $\mathbb{R}$

And the dimension of $E = \mathbb{R}^n$ is $dim_{\mathbb{R}}(E) = n$

Remark

The notion of matrices and the eigenvalues are also indispensable mathematics course applied on data analytics studies.

Complement of The Statistics Courses

Since the study of statistical analysis and knowledge in probability are essential during the practice of the method of data analytics, it is necessary to make a reminder of courses concerning these two disciplines.

The Descriptive Statistics

We suppose E a nonempty set $(E \neq O)$.

This set E is called the statistical population, and for every element x belonging to E, x is called an individual.

The present characteristic in each individual of E is denoted by C.

Finally, the set of values or observations of the characters is denoted by W.

49

By using mathematical notations, we have:

- $E \neq O$, designates the statistical population
- $\forall x, x \in E$, x is called individual.

Definitions

Statistical variable

The statistical variable associated with E to C is called the application:

$$X : E \rightarrow W$$
$$x \rightarrow w_i = X(x)$$

If the cardinal of W is finite or $W \subseteq \mathbb{N}$, we say that X is a discrete statistical variable.

If the set W is a part of $\mathbb{R}$, we say that X is a continuous statistical variable.

Example:

We assume that the character to be studied in each individual of a set E is the colors of eyes.

Let $C = Eye\ colors$, then $W = \{black,\ brown,\ blue\ ...\}$

Here $card(W)$ is finite, and then the variable statistic is defined as to be discrete.

Besides, if C is defined by the weights of individuals, then the set W is a part of $\mathbb{R}_+^*$ then the corresponding statistical variable is defined as to be continuous.

The Graphical Representation of a Statistical Variable

The statistical variable can be represented by several forms.

Example:

Graphical representation by sector: the statistical sector diagram

Graphical representation by histogram: the statistical bar plot or bar graphs, or histogram graphs etc.

Method of Frequency Calculation (f_i)

We suppose that $card(W)$ is finite. Let w_i be an element of W ($w_i \in W$) and n_i the numbers of individuals $x \in E$, such that $X(x) = w_i$.

We denote by f_i the absolute frequency of w_i for all the values of n_i, and we have:

$$f_i = \frac{n_i}{card(E)}$$

With this case, f_i is also called: the relative frequency of w_i.

Representations in diagrams

The line diagram

The line diagram is a graphical representation obtained by carrying each value $w_i \in W$ on a segment of length whose graph's form is given by $y = g_i(x)$.

The integral diagram

A function of distribution of X is any function F, such that

$$F: \mathbb{R} \to [0, 1]$$

that is defined by

$$F(x) = \sum_{1 < p < r} f_{p-1}$$

For all $x \in \,]x_{i-1}, x_i[$

The graph of F is called an integral diagram.

If x_i is the limit superior of the i-th partition of $I_i \in [1, n]$,

The distribution function of the continuous statistical variable X is the function $F\colon \mathbb{R} \to [0, 1]$ such that

$$F(x_i) = \sum_{1 < i < r} f_i$$

The diagram of X is the curve that connects the cordon points $[x_i, f(x_i)]$, $i \in [1, r]$.

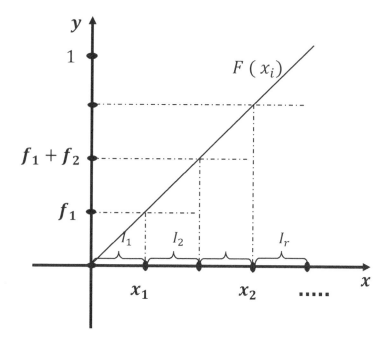

Note

The distribution of a statistical variable X is an increasing function, and is continuous on the left.

53

That means

$$\lim_{x \to -\infty} F(x) = 0 \text{ and } \lim_{x \to +\infty} F(x) = 1$$

Statistical Parameters Calculation

The mode

The mode is the element of W corresponding to the maximum frequency. We denote the mode by M_0.

The median

The median denoted by M_e is the solution of $F(x) = 1/2$, where F is the distribution function.

The arithmetic mean

The arithmetic mean is the number denoted by $\bar{x}$, such that

$$\bar{x} = \frac{1}{n} \sum n_i . x_i \text{ where } n = \sum n_i$$

Properties

If we have the equality, $M_0 = M_e = \bar{x}$,

- Then we say that the variable X has a symmetric distribution.

If we have the inequality, $M_0 < M_e < \bar{x}$,

- Then we say that the variable X has a symmetrical distribution spread to the right.

If we have the inequality, $M_0 > M_e > \bar{x}$,

- Then we say that the variable X has a symmetrical distribution spread to the left.

Variance and Centered Moment Calculation Method

The variance

Let X be a statistical variable. The variance of the variable X is called the number σ^2, such that

$$\sigma^2 = \frac{1}{n} \sum_{1 < i < p} (x_i - \bar{x})^2$$

i varying from 1 to p, p a positive integer.

The standard deviation

The standard deviation of the statistical variable X is the number denoted by σ, such as

$$\sigma = \sqrt{\frac{1}{n} \sum_{1 < i < p} (x_i - \bar{x})^2} = \sqrt{\sigma^2}$$

Consequently, we define the centered moment of order r by the quantity μ_r such that

$$\mu_r = \frac{1}{n} \sum_{1 < i < p} n_i(x_i - \bar{x})^2$$

i varying from 1 to p, p a positive integer.

Coefficient of variation

The coefficient of variation or relative standard deviation is the ratio of the mean to the standard deviation of the statistical variable.

That is

$$Cv = \frac{standard\ deviation}{mean} \times 100$$

This is similar to

$$Cv = \frac{\sigma}{\bar{x}} \times 100$$

The coefficient of variation Cv is used to compare two distributions.

The Quantile or Quartile Calculation

We denote by Q_1 the statistical parameter called first quartile. To calculate the first quartile, we must solve the equation $F(x) = \dfrac{1}{4}$

We denote by Q_3 the statistical parameter called the third quartile. To calculate the 3rd quartile, we must solve the equation $F(x) = \dfrac{3}{4}$

We denote by Q_2 the statistical parameter called 2nd quartile. To calculate the second quartile, we must solve the equation $F(x) = \dfrac{1}{2}$

The function F is the distribution function of the continuous statistic variable X.

Another Tests Used in Statistical Analysis

There exist several methods for accomplishing the different tests in Statistical analysis.

In our case, we will observe only the statistical test calculation method depending to the symmetry coefficients calculation.

Coefficient of symmetry of Fischer

This is the number defined by γ such that

$$\gamma = \frac{\mu_3}{\sigma^3}$$

Where σ the standard deviation and μ_3 is the centered moment of order 3

Coefficient of Pearson

This is the number denoted by d_1 such that

$$d_1 = \frac{\bar{x} - M_0}{\sigma}$$

- M_0 is the mode
- $\bar{x}$ is the arithmetic mean
- σ is the standard deviation

Coefficient of Yule

The coefficient of Yule is the number denoted by d_2 such that

$$d_2 = \frac{Q_1 + Q_2 - 2M_e}{\sigma}$$

- Q_1 is the statistical first quartile.
- Q_2 is the statistical second quartile.
- σ is the standard deviation.

Remarks

γ, d_1 and d_2 are dimensionless (no unit).
γ, d_1 and d_2 are positive if $M_0 < M_e < \bar{x}$

γ, d_1 and d_2 are negative if $M_0 > M_e > \bar{x}$

The Fischer flattening coefficient

The Fischer flattening coefficient is the number denoted by γ_e, such that

$$\gamma_e = [\frac{\mu_4}{\mu_2^2} - 3]$$

- μ_4 is the centered moment of order 4
- μ_2 is the centered moment of order 2

Chapter 5: Mathematical Statistics

Population and Sample

A statistical population is a non-empty homogeneous set E. According to what we have seen above, an element of E is called an individual.

Let $X: E \rightarrow R$ be a map of a random variable that schematizes a character C present in all individuals of E.

We call sample the element $(x_1, x_2, \dots, x_n)$ part of E, the n elements of the character C, the values taken respectively by n independent random variables X_1, $X_2, \dots, X_n$ having the same probability distribution.

Example:

$E = "population", C = "weight\ of\ an\ individual"$
$E = \{stores\}, C = "turnover"$
$E = "set\ of\ bulbs", C = "service\ life"$
X is called the parent random variable

Principle of Constitution of a Sample

A simple random sample is a sample such that its elements have been drawn at random.

With the sampling without replacement, it is said that the draw is exhaustive, otherwise replacement), the draw is said to be non-exhaustive, in which case, two successive draws must be made independent: an individual can be fired several times.

The Principal Purpose

After ordering, reducing and condensing the values of the character C of the sample, it is proposed to interpret C values, extend the properties of the sample to the parent population: evaluationof a risk of error that is encrypted in terms of probability.

Estimation and Estimator

Let X_1, X_2, ..., X_n be the sample of a character C. We assume that the probability distribution of the random variable X depends on a θ parameter.

We call the point estimate θ_n^* all functions T satisfying

$$T(x_1, x_2, ..., x_n) = \theta_n^*$$

The random variable $\widehat{\theta_n} = T(X_1, X_2, ..., X_n)$ is called the θ estimator.

In this case, the function T is called a decision function.

The Unbiased Estimator and Asymptotically Unbiased Estimator

We say that $\widehat{\theta_n}$ is an unbiased estimator of θ if

$$E\left(\widehat{\theta_n}\right) = \theta$$

In this case, an asymptotically unbiased estimator of θ is any $\widehat{\theta_n}$ estimator of θ such that

$$\lim_{n \to +\infty} E\left(\widehat{\theta_n}\right) = \theta$$

The difference $E\left(\widehat{\theta_n}\right) - \theta$ is called the bias of the $\widehat{\theta_n}$ estimator of θ.

The Convergent Estimator

Definitions

An unbiased estimator $\widehat{\theta_n}$ of θ is said to be a convergent estimator if

$$\lim_{n \to +\infty} V(\widehat{\theta_n}) = 0$$

V is a given variance.

An estimator that is both unbiased and convergent is called an absolutely correct estimator.

The Efficient Estimator

Let I be a non-empty set. We assume that I is the lower bound of the variances of the unbiased estimators of θ.

We say that $\widehat{\theta_n}$ is an efficient estimator of θ if $\widehat{\theta_n}$ is unbiased and if $V\left(\widehat{\theta_n}\right) = I$.

An efficient estimator does not always exist.

Notion of Probability Used in Data Analytics

The notion of probability is used as a one of the fundamental methods in data analytics process, by using the technique of the inferential statistics.

The Laws of a Probability of a Discrete Real Random Variable

Let $X(W) = \{x_1, x_2, \ldots x_n, \ldots\}$ be the set of the values of the discrete random variable X.

The real data p_i which verifies $P[X = xi] = P[\omega \in W/X(\omega) = x_i]$, defines the probability distribution of X, such that $p_i > 0$ $i = 1, \ldots, n$;   and $\sum_{1 < i < \infty} p_i = 1 = P(W)$.

Namely, for any random variable A,

we have

$$P[A] = \sum_{x_i \in A} p_i$$

$$= P[X \subseteq A].$$

63

We call the distribution function of the discrete real random variable X, the function

$$F: R \rightarrow [0,1]$$

$$x \rightarrow P[X < x] = \sum_{xi < x} pi .$$

This means that

$$F(x) = \sum_{xi < x} pi$$

$F(x)$ is continuous and is also an increasing function. In addition,

$$\lim_{x \rightarrow -\infty} F(x) = 0 \text{ and } \lim_{x \rightarrow +\infty} F(x) = 1$$

Mathematical Expectation of The Discrete Real Random Variable X

The mathematical expectation or the expected value of a discrete real random variable X is defined by

$$E[X] = \sum_{0 < i < +\infty} x_i P[X = x_i]$$

The Poisson's law

Let X be a discrete real random variable satisfying the condition

$$X: W \rightarrow N \subseteq R$$

The Poisson's law of this random variable is

$$P[X = n] = \frac{\lambda^n e^{-\lambda}}{n!}$$

The mathematical expectation of such a probability is equal to λ.

That means

$$E(X) = \lambda$$

For all real numbers $a, b \in \mathbb{R}^2$ we have

$$E(aX + b) = aE(X) + b$$

where X is a discrete real random variable.

The Poisson's law is also called the Poisson's law of small numbers.

The Markov's inequality

Let X be a discrete real random variable satisfying the condition

$$X: W \rightarrow \mathbb{R}^+$$

such that the value of $E(X)$ is finite,

then for all value of $\lambda > 0$, we have

$$P[X > \lambda] \leq \frac{E(X)}{\lambda}$$

This is the so-called Markov's inequality.

The Chebyshev's inequality

Let X be a discrete real random variable such that $\sigma^2 = V(X)$ the variance relative to X, whose value is finite.

We assume that $E(X) = m$, then the inequality of Chebyshev is the specific equality

$$P[|X - m| > \epsilon\sigma] \leq \frac{1}{\epsilon^2}$$

m is a finit expected value

The Centered and Reduced Random Variable

Let X and Y be two random variables. We say that the random variable Y is centered if the expectation of Y is equal to zero.

This means

$$\text{Y is centered if } E\left(Y\right) = 0$$

The variable Y is said to be reduced if the variance of Y is equal 1.

This means

$$\text{Y is reduced if } V\left(Y\right) = 1$$

Random Variable Absolutely Continuous

Overview

We say that the random variable X is absolutely continuous if

$$F\left(x\right) = P\left[X < x\right]$$

F is the distribution function of X

The distribution function of X is derivable and continuous function.

The expression $F'\left(x\right) = f\left(x\right)$ is in this case called the probability density of the random variable X.

Properties

Let F be the distribution function of X such that $F'\left(x\right) = f\left(x\right)$, then:

For every x element of $\mathbb{R}$, f (x)>= 0,

$$F(x) = P[X \leq x]$$

For each element $(a, b) \in \mathbb{R} \times \mathbb{R}$

$$P[X = a] = 0$$

And

$$P[a < X < b] = P[a \leq X \leq b] = P[a \leq X < b] = P[a < X \leq b]$$

And in addition

$$\lim_{x \to -\infty} F(x) = 0 \text{ and } \lim_{x \to +\infty} F(x) = 1$$

The Uniform Law Over a Set $[a, b]$

Let X be an absolute random variable. We say that the law of probability of X is the uniform law on a set $[a, b]$, if it has the probability density:

$$F(x) = \begin{cases} \dfrac{1}{b-a} & \text{for } x \in [a, b] \\ 0 & \text{for } x \notin [a, b] \end{cases}$$

Its function of distribution is defined by the function F such that

$$F(x) = \int_a^x \frac{dt}{b-a}$$

This value is also equal to $F(x) = \frac{x-a}{b-a}$

If $\notin [a, b]$, for all value of $x \leq a$ then

$$F(x) = \int_{-\infty}^x \frac{dt}{b-a} = 0$$

If $\notin [a, b]$, for all value of $x > a$ then

$$F(x) = \int_a^b \frac{dt}{b-a} = 1$$

Normal and Reduced Normal Law (Gauss or Laplace-Gauss's Law)

We say that the random variable absolutely continuous X has a probability law the normal centered law and reduced, if its probability density is given by

$$f(x) = \frac{1}{\sqrt{2\pi}} e^{\frac{-x^2}{2}}$$

Its distribution function is therefore

$$F\,(x) = P[X < x] = \int_{-\infty}^{x} \frac{dt}{b-a}$$

and we know that $\lim\limits_{x \to +\infty} F\,(x) = 1$

therefore

$$\int_{-\infty}^{+\infty} \frac{1}{\sqrt{2\pi}} \, e^{\frac{-t^2}{2}} \, dt = 1$$

And this implies the value of the integral $\int_{-\infty}^{+\infty} e^{\frac{-t^2}{2}} \, dt$

That is $\int_{-\infty}^{+\infty} \frac{1}{\sqrt{2\pi}} \, e^{\frac{-t^2}{2}} \, dt = \frac{1}{\sqrt{2\pi}} \int_{-\infty}^{+\infty} e^{\frac{-t^2}{2}} \, dt = 1$ and from where

$$\int_{-\infty}^{+\infty} e^{\frac{-t^2}{2}} \, dt = \sqrt{2\pi}$$

The normal centered and reduced normal law can be abbreviated by $N\,(0,1)$.

Normal Distribution $N\,(m, \sigma^2)$

We suppose that X is an absolute random variable. We say that the probability law of X is the normal distribution $N(m, \sigma^2)$ if X has the probability density

$$f(x) = \frac{1}{\sigma\sqrt{2\pi}} \, e^{\frac{-(x-m)^2}{2\sigma^2}}$$

σ^2 is the covariance and m is the mathematical expectation of X.

Its distribution function is given by

$$F(x) = P[X < x] =$$

$$= \int_{-\infty}^{X} \frac{1}{\sigma\sqrt{2\pi}} \, e^{\frac{-(t-m)^2}{2\sigma^2}} \, dt$$

The Mathematical expectation of an absolutely continuous random variable

Definition

We call the mathematical expectation of an absolute random variable with a density of probability f, the quantity defined by

$$E(x) = \int_{-\infty}^{+\infty} x \, f(x) \, dx$$

The Discrete Random Vectors

We call a random vector of dimension Z of dimension $n, n > 1$,
the map $Z: W \rightarrow \mathbb{R}^n$

for all $(x_1, x_2, \ldots, x_n)$ element of $\mathbb{R}^n$, and that $Z = (X_1, X_2, \ldots, X_n)$

Law of probability of a discrete random vector

Let $Z = (X, Y)$ be a discrete random vector.

We assume that $X = (x_1, x_2, \ldots, x_n)$ and that $Y = (y_1, y_2, \ldots, y_n)$

Then

$$P[X = x_n, Y = y_n] = P[(Y = yk)].P[(Y = yk)]$$
$$= P[(X = x_n) \cap (Y = y_n)]$$

such that for every n element of $\mathbb{N}^*$ for any k element of $\mathbb{N}^*$

$$p_{nk} \geq 0,$$

And

$$\sum_{n \geq 1} \sum_{k \geq 1} p_{nk} = 1$$

72

defines the probability distribution of Z

Law of Marginal Probability

For all value of (n, k) element of $\mathbb{N}^* \times \mathbb{N}^*$, $p_{nk} \geq 0$ is considered as a double sequence.

If $p_{nk} \geq 0$, (n, k) element of $\mathbb{N}^* \times \mathbb{N}^*$ defines the law of probability of $Z = (X, Y)$, then we have the following equations

$$P[X = x_n] = \sum_{k \geq 1} p_{nk} = 1$$

And

$$P[Y = y_n] = \sum_{n \geq 1} p_{kn} = 1$$

The Contingency Table

Let $Z = (X, Y)$ be a discrete random vector.

We assume that $X = (x_1, x_2, \dots, x_n)$ and that $Y = (y_1, y_2, \dots, y_n)$

The contingency table is the double entry table for grouping the values p_{nk}, and to observe the two marginal laws represented by the random vector Z.

Conclusion

We have developed in some paragraphs of this book the different steps to follow in order to start studying a data analytics task, as well as some process to follow and design concerning the practice of this new method.

Even if a course was offered for a perfect guide for the beginners of that most used discipline, we have as well mentioned the advantages, and above all, the importance of its integration in the various fields or sectors of activity.

This method is really up to date, stylish, popular and also so smart.
At present, the practice of the method of data analytics and statistical analysis allows operators or enterprise developers to promote their current tasks, their production techniques and to foresee the different circumstances concerning their activities.

Moreover, it can be said that the method of data analytics ranks first among the different tools and techniques used by companies or production industries, companies or commercial activities, to accomplish the various activities.

The experts in data analytics, called data analysts have the full decisions, while the operators or promoters are only performing their advice.

Currently, the raw materials whose companies as public entities, schools, universities use are formed by collecting digital data, because of the distribution of computerization.

The processing and exploration of these data requires a rational technique, relevant and above all well-organized.

To meet our needs, we have introduced the method of statistical analysis, considered as a fundamental tool of all kinds of analysis, satisfying requirements of international standards for the promotion of any field of studies and sector of activities.

Besides, the notion of probability cannot be neglected in the practice of this method because among the various laws proposed by this discipline, it is possible to explain certain problems concerning the inferential statistical analysis.

Finally, the accomplishment of the data analytics method is made by the use of some mathematical and computer science skills (specific software), on which all the applied theories to this new technique are based.

Last Chance to Get YOUR Bonus!

FOR A LIMITED TIME ONLY – Get the best-selling book *"5 Steps to Learn Absolutely Anything in as Little As 3 Days!"* by TeachingNerds absolutely FREE!

Readers who have read this bonus book as well have seen huge increases in their abilities to learn new things and apply it to their lives – so it is *highly recommended* to get this bonus book.

Once again, as a big thank-you for downloading this book, I'd like to offer it to you *100% FREE for a LIMITED TIME ONLY!*

To download your FREE copy, go to:

TeachingNerds.com/Bonus

Final Words

I would like to thank you for downloading my book and I hope I have been able to help you and educate you on something new.

If you have enjoyed this book and would like to share your positive thoughts, could you please take 30 seconds of your time to go back and give me a review on my Amazon book page!

I greatly appreciate seeing these reviews because it helps me share my hard work!

Again, thank you and I wish you all the best!

Disclaimer

This book and related sites provide information in an informative and educational manner only, with information that is general in nature and that is not specific to you, the reader. The contents of this site are intended to assist you and other readers in your education efforts. Consult an expert regarding the applicability of any information provided in our books and sites to you.

Nothing in this book should be construed as personal advice, legal advice, or expert advice, and must not be used in this manner. The information provided is general in nature. This information does not cover all possible uses, actions, precautions, consequences, etc. such as loss of data or hardware failure.

You should consult with an expert before applying anything in this book. This book should not be used in place of learning from a professional or seeking advice from a technical specialist.

No Warranties: The authors and publishers don't guarantee or warrant the quality, accuracy, completeness, timeliness, appropriateness or suitability of the information in this book, or of any product or services referenced by this book, other books, and websites.

The information in this book and on relevant websites is provided on an "as is" basis and the authors and publishers make no representations or warranties of any kind with respect to this information. This site may contain inaccuracies, typographical errors, or other errors.

Liability Disclaimer: The publishers, authors, and other parties involved in the creation, production, provision of information, or delivery of this book and related websites specifically disclaim any responsibility, and shall not be held liable for any damages, claims, injuries, losses, liabilities, costs, or obligations including any direct, indirect, special, incidental, or consequences damages (collectively known as "Damages") whatsoever and howsoever caused, arising out of, or in connection with the use or misuse of the site and the information contained within it, whether such Damages arise in contract, tort, negligence, equity, statute law, or by way of other legal theory.

CPSIA information can be obtained
at www.ICGtesting.com
Printed in the USA
FSHW011956291219
65564FS